HEIAN, TEKKI

BEST KARATE 5

Heian, Tekki

M. Nakayama

KODANSHA INTERNATIONAL
Tokyo • New York • London

Front cover photo by Keizō Kaneko; demonstration photos by Yoshinao Murai.

Distributed in the United States by Kodansha America, Inc., 114 Fifth Avenue, New York, N.Y. 10011, and in the United Kingdom and continental Europe by Kodansha Europe Ltd., 95 Aldwych, London WC2B 4JF. Published by Kodansha International Ltd., 17-14 Otowa 1-chome, Bunkyo-ku, Tokyo 112, and Kodansha America, Inc. Copyright © 1979 by Kodansha International Ltd. All rights reserved. Printed in Japan.

LCC 77-74829
ISBN 0-87011-379-8
ISBN 4-7700-0726-4 (in Japan)

First edition, 1979
93 94 95 20 19 18 17 16 15

CONTENTS

Introduction   9
What Karate-dō Is   11
Kata   12
  Meaning, Important Points, Heian and Tekki
Heian 1   15
  Important Points, 28
Heian 2   31
  Important Points, 46
Heian 3   49
  Important Points, 60
Heian 4   63
  Important Points, 74
Heian 5   77
  Important Points, 90
Tekki 1   93
  Important Points, 106
Tekki 2   109
  Important Points, 121
Tekki 3   123
  Important Points, 140
Glossary   142

Dedicated
to my teacher
GICHIN FUNAKOSHI

The past decade has seen a great increase in the popularity of karate-dō throughout the world. Among those who have been attracted to it are college students and teachers, artists, businessmen and civil servants. It has come to be practiced by policemen and members of Japan's Self-defense Forces. In a number of universities, it has become a compulsory subject, and that number is increasing yearly.

Along with the increase in popularity, there have been certain unfortunate and regrettable interpretations and performances. For one thing, karate has been confused with the so-called Chinese-style boxing, and its relationship with the original Okinawan *Te* has not been sufficiently understood. There are also people who have regarded it as a mere show, in which two men attack each other savagely, or the contestants battle each other as though it were a form of boxing in which the feet are used, or a man shows off by breaking bricks or other hard objects with his head, hand or foot.

If karate is practiced solely as a fighting technique, this is cause for regret. The fundamental techniques have been developed and perfected through long years of study and practice, but to make any effective use of these techniques, the spiritual aspect of this art of self-defense must be recognized and must play the predominant role. It is gratifying to me to see that there are those who understand this, who know that karate-dō is a purely Oriental martial art, and who train with the proper attitude.

To be capable of inflicting devastating damage on an opponent with one blow of the fist or a single kick has indeed been the objective of this ancient Okinawan martial art. But even the practitioners of old placed stronger emphasis on the spiritual side of the art than on the techniques. Training means training of body and spirit, and, above all else, one should treat his opponent courteously and with the proper etiquette. It is not enough to fight with all one's power; the real objective in karate-dō is to do so for the sake of justice.

Gichin Funakoshi, a great master of karate-dō, pointed out repeatedly that the first purpose in pursuing this art is the nurturing of a sublime spirit, a spirit of humility. Simultaneously, power sufficient to destroy a ferocious wild animal with a single blow should be developed. Becoming a true follower of karate-dō is possible only when one attains perfection in these two aspects, the one spiritual, the other physical.

Karate as an art of self-defense and karate as a means of improving and maintaining health has long existed. During the past twenty years, a new activity has been explored and is coming to the fore. This is *sports karate.*

In sports karate, contests are held for the purpose of determining the ability of the participants. This needs emphasizing, for here again there is cause for regret. There is a tendency to place too much emphasis on winning contests, and those who do so neglect the practice of fundamental techniques, opting instead to attempt jiyū kumite at the earliest opportunity.

Emphasis on winning contests cannot help but alter the fundamental techniques a person uses and the practice he engages in. Not only that, it will result in a person's being incapable of executing a strong and effective technique, which, after all, is the unique characteristic of karate-dō. The man who begins jiyū kumite prematurely—without having practiced fundamentals sufficiently—will soon be overtaken by the man who has trained in the basic techniques long and diligently. It is, quite simply, a matter of haste makes waste. There is no alternative to learning and practicing basic techniques and movements step by step, stage by stage.

If karate competitions are to be held, they must be conducted under suitable conditions and in the proper spirit. The desire to win a contest is counterproductive, since it leads to a lack of seriousness in learning the fundamentals. Moreover, aiming for a savage display of strength and power in a contest is totally undesirable. When this happens, courtesy toward the opponent is forgotten, and this is of prime importance in any expression of karate. I believe this matter deserves a great deal of reflection and self-examination by both instructors and students.

To explain the many and complex movements of the body, it has been my desire to present a fully illustrated book with an up-to-date text, based on the experience in this art that I have acquired over a period of forty-six years. This hope is being realized by the publication of the *Best Karate* series, in which earlier writings of mine have been totally revised with the help and encouragement of my readers. This new series explains in detail what karate-dō is in language made as simple as possible, and I sincerely hope that it will be of help to followers of karate-dō. I hope also that karateka in many countries will be able to understand each other better through this series of books.

WHAT KARATE-DŌ IS

Deciding who is the winner and who is the loser is not the ultimate objective. Karate-dō is a martial art for the development of character through training, so that the karateka can surmount any obstacle, tangible or intangible.

Karate-dō is an empty-handed art of self-defense in which the arms and legs are systematically trained and an enemy attacking by surprise can be controlled by a demonstration of strength like that of using actual weapons.

Karate-dō is exercise through which the karateka masters all body movements, such as bending, jumping and balancing, by learning to move limbs and body backward and forward, left and right, up and down, freely and uniformly.

The techniques of karate-dō are well controlled according to the karateka's will power and are directed at the target accurately and spontaneously.

The essence of karate techniques is *kime*. The meaning of *kime* is an explosive attack to the target using the appropriate technique and maximum power in the shortest time possible. (Long ago, there was the expression *ikken hissatsu*, meaning "to kill with one blow," but to assume from this that killing is the objective is dangerous and incorrect. It should be remembered that the karateka of old were able to practice *kime* daily and in dead seriousness by using the makiwara.)

Kime may be accomplished by striking, punching or kicking, but also by blocking. A technique lacking *kime* can never be regarded as true karate, no matter how great the resemblance to karate. A contest is no exception; however, it is against the rules to make contact because of the danger involved.

Sun-dome means to arrest a technique just before contact with the target (one *sun*, about three centimeters). But not carrying a technique through to *kime* is not true karate, so the question is how to reconcile the contradiction between *kime* and *sun-dome*. The answer is this: establish the target slightly in front of the opponent's vital point. It can then be hit in a controlled way with maximum power, without making contact.

Training transforms various parts of the body into weapons to be used freely and effectively. The quality necessary to accomplish this is self-control. To become a victor, one must first overcome his own self.

KATA

The *kata* of karate-dō are logical arrangements of blocking, punching, striking and kicking techniques in certain set sequences. About fifty kata, or "formal exercises," are practiced at the present time, some having been passed down from generation to generation, others having been developed fairly recently.

Kata can be divided into two broad categories. In one group are those appropriate for physical development, the strengthening of bone and muscle. Though seemingly simple, they require composure for their performance and exhibit strength and dignity when correctly performed. In the other group are kata suitable for the development of fast reflexes and the ability to move quickly. The lightninglike movements in these kata are suggestive of the rapid flight of the swallow. All kata require and foster rhythm and coordination.

Training in kata is spiritual as well as physical. In his performance of the kata, the karateka should exhibit boldness and confidence, but also humility, gentleness and a sense of decorum, thus integrating mind and body in a singular discipline. As Gichin Funakoshi often reminded his students, "The spirit of karate-dō is lost without courtesy."

One expression of this courtesy is the bow made at the beginning and at the end of each kata. The stance is the *musubi-dachi* (informal attention stance), with the arms relaxed, the hands lightly touching the thighs and the eyes focused straight ahead.

From the bow at the start of the kata, one moves into the *kamae* of the first movement of the kata. This is a relaxed position, so tenseness, particularly in the shoulders and knees, should be eliminated and breathing should be relaxed. The center of power and concentration is the *tanden*, the center of gravity. In this position, the karateka should be prepared for any eventuality and full of fighting spirit.

Being relaxed but alert also characterizes the bow at the end of the kata and is called *zanshin*. In karate-dō, as in other martial arts, bringing the kata to a perfect finish is of the greatest importance.

Each kata begins with a blocking technique and consists of a specific number of movements to be performed in a particular order. There is some variation in the complexity of the movements and the time required to complete them, but each movement has its own meaning and function and nothing is superfluous. Performance is along the *embusen* (performance line), the shape of which is decided for each kata.

While performing a kata, the karateka should imagine himself to be surrounded by opponents and be prepared to execute defensive and offensive techniques in any direction.

Mastery of kata is a prerequisite for advancement through *kyū* and *dan* as follows:

8th *kyū*	Heian 1
7th *kyū*	Heian 2
6th *kyū*	Heian 3
5th *kyū*	Heian 4
4th *kyū*	Heian 5
3rd *kyū*	Tekki 1
2nd *kyū*	Kata other than Heian or Tekki
1st *kyū*	Other than the above
1st *dan*	Other than the above
2nd *dan* and above	Free kata

Free kata may be chosen from Bassai, Kankū, Jitte, Hangetsu, Empi, Gankaku, Jion, Tekki, Nijūshihō, Gojūshihō, Unsu, Sōchin, Meikyō, Chintei, Wankan and others.

Important Points

Since the effects of practice are cumulative, practice every day, even if only for a few minutes. When performing a kata, keep calm and never rush through the movements. This means always being aware of the correct timing of each movement. If a particular kata proves difficult, give it more attention, and always keep in mind the relationship between kata practice and kumite (see Vols. 3 and 4).

Specific points in performance are:

1. *Correct order*. The number and sequence of movements is predetermined. All must be performed.

2. *Beginning and end*. The kata must begin and end at the same spot on the *embusen*. This requires practice.

3. *Meaning of each movement*. Each movement, defensive or offensive must be clearly understood and fully expressed. This is also true of the kata as a whole, each of which has its own characteristics.

4. *Awareness of the target*. The karateka must know what the target is and when to execute a technique.

5. *Rhythm and timing*. Rhythm must be appropriate to the particular kata and the body must be flexible, never overstrained. Remember the three factors of the correct use of power, swiftness or slowness in executing techniques, and the stretching and contraction of muscles.

6. *Proper breathing*. Breathing should change with changing situations, but basically inhale when blocking, exhale

when a finishing technique is executed, and inhale and exhale when executing successive techniques.

Related to breathing is the *kiai*, which occurs in the middle or at the end of the kata, at the moment of maximum tension. By exhaling very sharply and tensing the abdomen, extra power can be given to the muscles.

Heian and Tekki

The five Heian and three Tekki kata are all basic kata.

Through the performance of the Heian kata, one should master the principles and skills that are indispensable in karate.

From the Tekki kata, one should acquire the dignity and strength of karate techniques, but more than that, he should come to master the dynamic, driving force that comes through practice designed to make the hips and stances strong.

The *embusen* in Heian 1 and 2 is I shaped. In Heian 3 and 5, it is T shaped. In Heian 4, it is shaped like an I, but with the vertical line extending above the upper horizontal line.

The *embusen* in the Tekki kata is a straight line.

HEIAN 1

From bow to shizen-tai

Move left foot first.

2 Migi chūdan oi-zuki

Right middle level lunge punch Keep left foot firm. Punch
while sliding right foot forward.

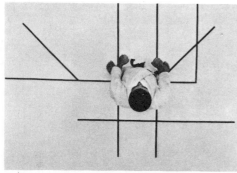

Shizen-tai. Hachinoji-dachi

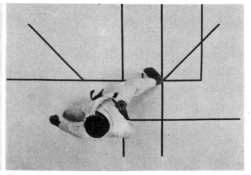

1. Hidari zenkutsu-dachi

1 *Hidari gedan barai*

Left downward block   The left fist should be about 15 centimeters above the left knee.

3 *Migi gedan barai*

Right downward block   Left leg is *jiku ashi* (pivot leg). Move right leg in a wide arc.

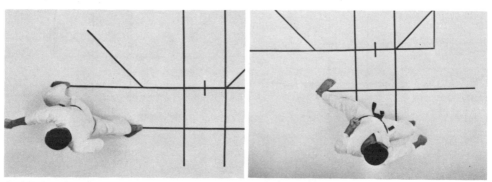

2. *Migi zenkutsu-dachi*   3. *Migi zenkutsu-dachi*

4 *Migi kentsui tate mawashi-uchi*

Vertical strike with right hammer fist First bring right foot halfway back and right fist back strongly. Advance right foot

5 *Hidari chūdan oi-zuki*

Left middle level lunge punch Slide left foot one step forward. Tighten right leg.

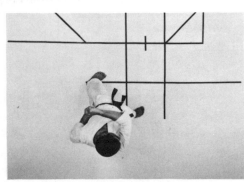 

4. *Migi zenkutsu-dachi*

and strike. No power in elbow. Twist right arm so back of fist is to the right.

<table>
<tr><td>6</td><td>Hidari gedan barai</td></tr>
</table>

Left downward block Right leg is *jiku ashi*. Turn hips to left. Slide left foot to left.

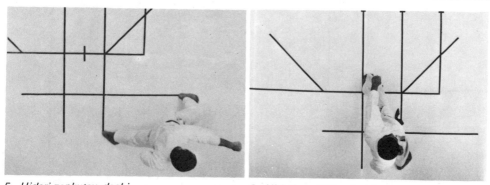

5. *Hidari zenkutsu-dachi*

6. *Hidari zenkutsu-dachi*

7 Migi jōdan age-uke

Right upper level rising block   Cross left palm and right forearm in front of jaw. Slide right foot forward. Twist right forearm so back of fist is to the rear.

8 Hidari jōdan age-uke

Left upper level rising block   Open and close right fist. Bring it to the right hip.

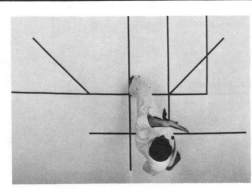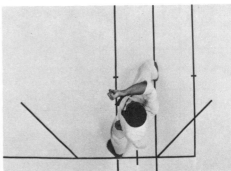

7. *Migi zenkutsu-dachi*

9 *Migi jōdan age-uke*

EI!

Right upper level rising block hand outward. Cross wrists.

Open and close left fist, back of

8. *Hidari zenkutsu-dachi*

9. *Migi zenkutsu-dachi*

10 Hidari gedan barai

Left downward block   Raise left fist to right shoulder. Pivot to the left.

12 Migi gedan barai

Right downward block   With left leg as *jiku ashi*, turn hips to the right.

10. *Hidari zenkutsu-dachi*   11. *Migi zenkutsu-dachi*

11 *Migi chūdan oi-zuki*

Right middle level lunge punch Slide right foot forward.
Tighten left leg.

13 *Hidari chūdan oi-zuki*

Left middle level lunge punch Slide left foot forward. Tighten
right leg.

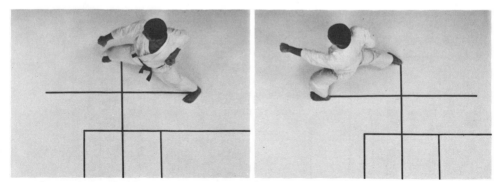

12. Migi zenkutsu-dachi　　　*13. Hidari zenkutsu-dachi*

14 *Hidari gedan barai*

Left downward block   Turn hips to left, move left leg to left.

16 *Hidari chūdan oi-zuki*

Left middle level lunge punch   Slide left foot one step forward.

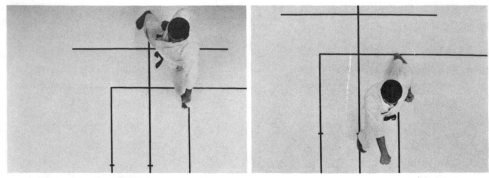

14. *Hidari zenkutsu-dachi*   15. *Migi zenkutsu-dachi*

15 *Migi chūdan oi-zuki*

Right middle level lunge punch   Slide right foot one step forward.

17 *Migi chūdan oi-zuki*

Right middle level lunge punch   Slide right foot one step forward.

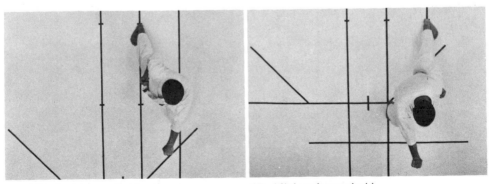

16. *Hidari zenkutsu-dachi*   17. *Migi zenkutsu-dachi*

18 Hidari shutō uke

Left sword hand block Turn with right knee bent. Bring left leg to left side.

20 Migi shutō uke

Right sword hand block Keep left knee bent and pivot on left leg to the right.

18. *Migi kōkutsu-dachi*

19. *Hidari kōkutsu-dachi*

19 *Migi shutō uke*

Right sword hand block With left knee bent, shift body weight to left leg.

21 *Hidari shutō uke*   *Yame*

Left sword hand block Shift weight to right leg gradually. Turn diagonally to left.

Clench both fists and bring back left foot.

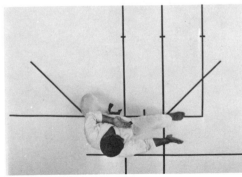

20. *Hidari kōkutsu-dachi*

21. *Migi kōkutsu-dachi*

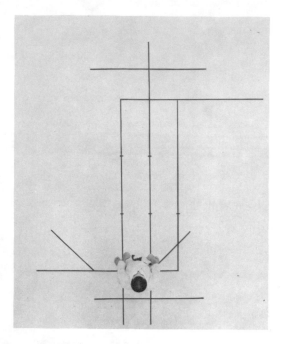

Heian 1 is composed of basic blocking techniques—downward block, upper level rising block, middle level block with the back of the sword hand—and the middle level straight punch. The stances are the front stance and the back stance. Also included is the method of countering when your wrist is grasped by a strong opponent. The most important things to master in this kata are reversing direction and leg movements.

Twenty-one movements. About forty seconds.

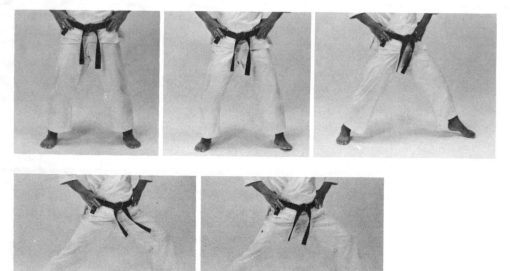

1

1. To execute a technique to the left side from *shizen-tai*, turn hips to the left, slide left foot to the left.

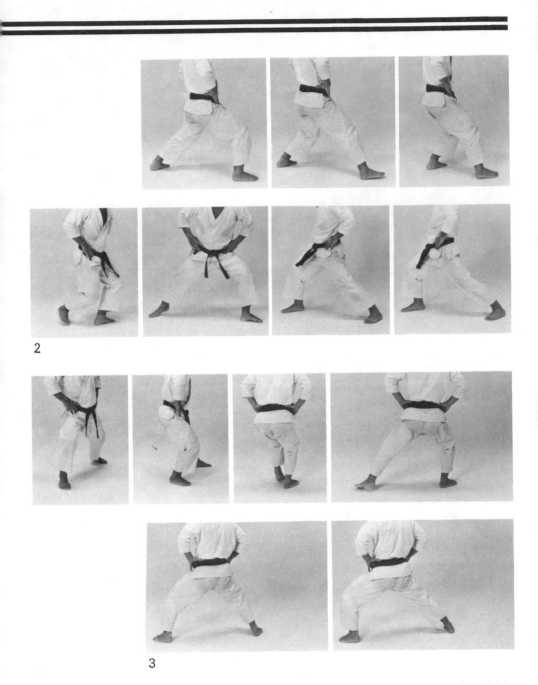

2. In reversing direction, the feeling should be of quickly pulling the hips toward the heel of the pivot leg. Do not raise the heel of the pivot foot.

3. In circling to the right side with right leg as pivot, quickly rotate hips to the left and quickly slide left foot.

4

5

4. In reversing direction, use the right front leg of the front stance as the pivot leg. Turn hips to the left to take a left back stance to the right side. Bend right knee; do not change height of hips.

5. In going from back stance to back stance, shift weight to front leg. Slide back leg forward or to the side.

HEIAN $\frac{2}{2}$

1 *Hidari haiwan hidari sokumen jōdan yoko uke*
Migi zenwan hitai mae yoko kamae

Upper level block to left side with left back-arm/Right forearm at side of forehead kamae

3 *Hidari ken hidari sokumen chūdan-zuki*
Migi ken migi koshi kamae

Middle level punch to left side with left fist/Right fist at right side

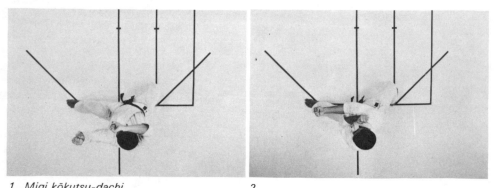

1. *Migi kōkutsu-dachi*　　　　　　2.

2
Migi kentsui hidari sokumen uchi-komi
Hidari tekubi nagashi-uke

Strike to left side with right hammer fist/Sweeping block with
left wrist

4
Migi haiwan migi sokumen jōdan yoko uke
Hidari zenwan hitai mae yoko kamae

Upper level block to right side with right back-arm/Left forearm
at side of forehead kamae

3.

4. Hidari kōkutsu-dachi

5 Hidari kentsui migi sokumen uchi-komi
Migi tekubi nagashi-uke

Strike to right side with left hammer fist/Sweeping block with right wrist

7 a Hidari ken ue migi ken

Right fist on top of left fist   Turn hips to right. Raise right sole to left knee.

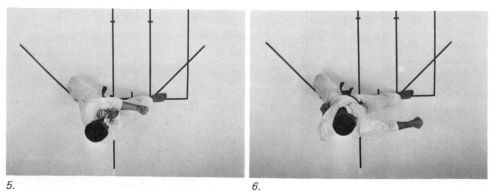

5.   6.

6 *Migi ken migi sokumen chūdan-zuki*
Hidari ken hidari koshi

Middle level punch to right side with right fist/Left fist at left side

7 b *Migi uraken jōdan yoko mawashi-uchi*
Migi sokutō yoko keage

Upper level horizontal strike with right back-fist/Side snap kick with right sword foot

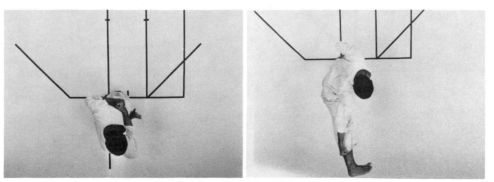

7a. *Hidari ashi-dachi*   7b.

8 *Hidari shutō uke*
Migi shutō suigetsu mae kamae

Left sword hand block/Right sword hand in front of chest kamae
Return kicking foot smoothly.

10 *Hidari shutō uke*

Left sword hand block Slide left foot one step forward.

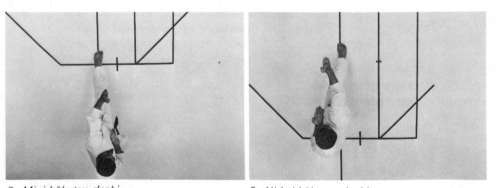

8. *Migi kōkutsu-dachi*   9. *Hidari kōkutsu-dachi*

Migi shutō uke

Right sword hand block Shift weight to left leg, bend left knee, slide right foot forward.

11 Migi shihon nukite chūdan tate-zuki Hidari shō osae-uke

EI!

Middle level vertical punch with right four-finger spear hand/Pressing block with left palm

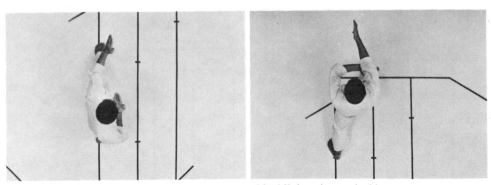

10. Migi kōkutsu-dachi

11. Migi zenkutsu-dachi

12 Hidari shutō uke

Left sword hand block With right leg as pivot, rotate hips in a wide movement to the left.

14 Migi shutō uke

Right sword hand block Left leg is pivot leg. Rotate hips to the right.

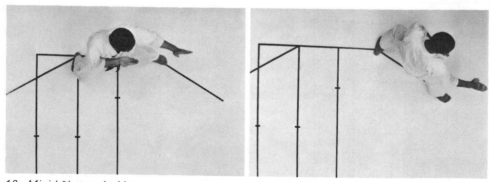

12. *Migi kōkutsu-dachi* 13. *Hidari kōkutsu-dachi*

13 *Migi shutō uke*

Right sword hand block Shift weight to left leg. Slide right foot
diagonally forward.

15 *Hidari shutō uke*

Left sword hand block Shift weight to right leg and slide left
foot diagonally forward.

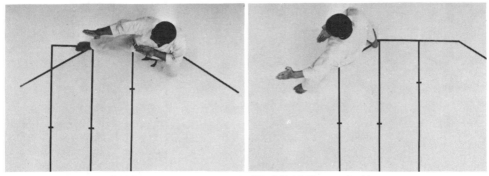

14. *Hidari kōkutsu-dachi*   15. *Migi kōkutsu-dachi*

16 Migi chūdan uchi uke
Gyaku hanmi

Right middle level block, inside outward/Reverse half-front-facing position

18 Hidari ken chūdan gyaku-zuki

Middle level reverse punch with left fist Punch as soon as kicking foot returns to floor.

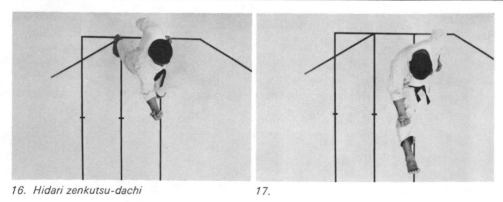

16. *Hidari zenkutsu-dachi*   17.

17 *Migi mae keage*

Right front snap kick   Execute techniques 16, 17 and 18 rapidly.

19 *Hidari chūdan uchi uke*

Left middle level block, inside outward   Turning hips brings right foot half a step back automatically.

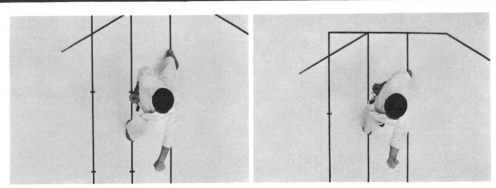

18. *Migi zenkutsu-dachi*   19.

20 *Hidari mae keage*

Left front snap kick   Execute techniques 19, 20 and 21 rapidly.

22 *Migi chūdan morote uke (Migi chūdan uchi uke/ Hidari ken migi empi yoko-zoe)*

Right middle level augmented forearm block (Right middle level block, inside outward/Left fist at right elbow)

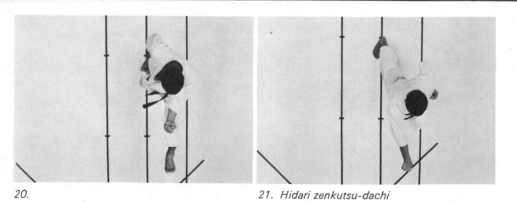

20.

21. *Hidari zenkutsu-dachi*

21 *Migi ken chūdan gyaku-zuki*

Middle level reverse punch with right fist Punch while taking front stance after kick.

 23 *Hidari gedan barai*

Left downward block Right leg is pivot leg. Rotate hips to the left.

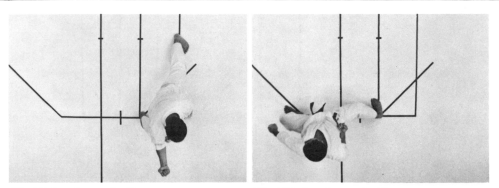

22. *Migi zenkutsu-dachi*   23. *Hidari zenkutsu-dachi*

24 | Migi jōdan age-uke

Right upper level rising block
Open left hand, bring it to the jaw, then advance left foot.

26 | Hidari jōdan age-uke

Left upper level rising block Advance left foot, block,
withdraw other hand at the same time.

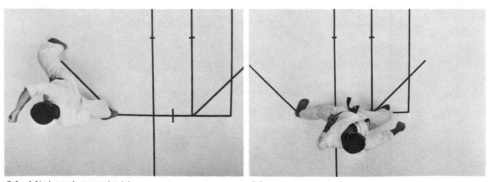

24. Migi zenkutsu-dachi   *25. Migi zenkutsu-dachi*

Migi gedan barai

Right downward block With left leg as pivot, rotate hips in a
wide movement.

Yame

Return to *shizen-tai* by withdrawing left foot.

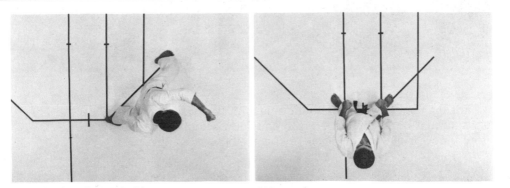

26. *Hidari zenkutsu-dachi*   *Shizen-tai*

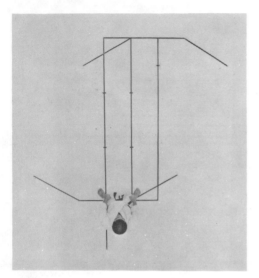

Techniques practiced in Heian 2 are the upper level block to the side with the upperside of the forearm, front kick, and simultaneous attack with side kick and back-fist. For this simultaneous attack to be strong and effective, the *kamae* in movement 7 must be perfect. It is also important to perfectly master reversing directions and taking the reverse half-front-facing position starting from the same position.

Twenty-six movements. About forty seconds.

1

1. For the upper level block to the side with the back-arm, the arms should be in the same plane and form a rectangle. The front elbow is at shoulder level, the back elbow at ear level.

2

2. For the simultaneous back-fist strike-side kick, form an axis with the supporting leg, hips and head. Raise the kicking foot to the other knee while turning the hips.

3

3. Executing a technique from *gyaku hanmi*: With the right leg
as pivot, block inside outward with the right arm at the same
time the hips are turned to the left and the left leg advances.
Do this by thrusting the right hip forward, *not* by taking a big
step with the left leg.
Reverse punch and inside-outward block after front kick:
When blocking, the front leg automatically comes back half a
step. Do not consciously pull it back.

$$\frac{3}{\text{HEIAN } 3}$$

1 *Hidari ken hidari sokumen chūdan uchi uke*
Migi ken migi koshi

Middle level block, inside outward, to left side with left fist/Right fist at right side

3 *Hidari chūdan uchi uke*
Migi gedan uke

Left middle level block, inside outward/Right downward block
Execute techniques 2 and 3 rapidly.

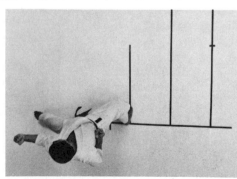

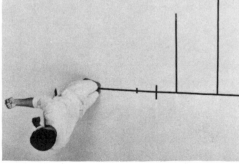

1. Migi kōkutsu-dachi

2. Heisoku-dachi

2 *Migi chūdan uchi uke*
Hidari gedan uke

Right middle level block, inside outward/Left downward block
Bring right fist outside left elbow.

4 *Migi chūdan uchi uke*

Right middle level block, inside outward   Rotate hips in a wide
movement.

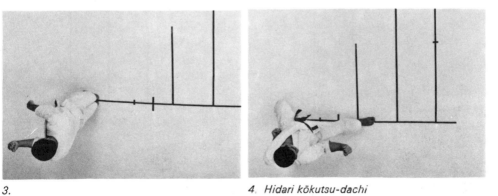

3.

4. *Hidari kōkutsu-dachi*

5 *Hidari chūdan uchi uke*
Migi gedan uke

Left middle level block, inside outward/Right downward block
Cross arms in front of chest.

7 *Hidari chūdan morote uke (Hidari chūdan uchi*
uke/ Migi ken hidari empi yoko-zoe)

Left middle level augmented forearm block (Left middle level
block, inside outward/Right fist at left elbow)

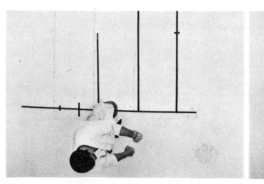

5. *Heisoku-dachi*   6.

6 Migi chūdan uchi uke
Hidari gedan uke

Right middle level block, inside outward/Left downward block
Execute 5 and 6 rapidly.

8 Migi nukite chūdan tate-zuki
Hidari shō osae-uke

Middle level vertical punch with right spear hand/Pressing block
with left palm

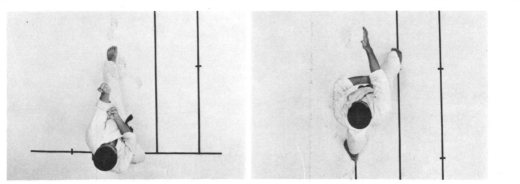

7. Migi kōkutsu-dachi

8. Mıgi zenkutsu-dachi

9 Hidari kentsui chūdan yoko mawashi-uchi

Middle level horizontal strike with left hammer fist   Back of left fist upward.

11 Ryō ken ryō koshi kamae

Both fists at the sides kamae   Rotate hips to left slowly. Slide left foot next to right foot.

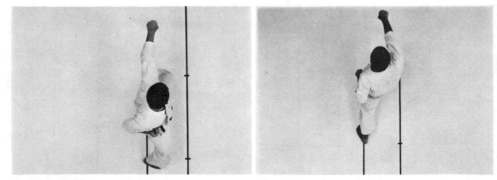

9. *Kiba-dachi*   10. *Migi zenkutsu-dachi*

10 *Migi chūdan oi-zuki*

Right middle level lunge punch Execute techniques 9 and 10 rapidly.

12 *Migi empi yoko uchi*
Jōtai sono mama

Side strike with right elbow/Upper body as before Rotate hips quickly to the left.

11. Heisoku-dachi

12. Kiba-dachi

13 *Migi uraken migi sokumen tate mawashi-uchi*

Vertical strike to right side with right back-fist Return right fist to right hip after strike.

15 *Hidari uraken hidari sokumen tate mawashi-uchi*

Vertical strike to left side with left back-fist Strike in a semi-circle starting from jaw.

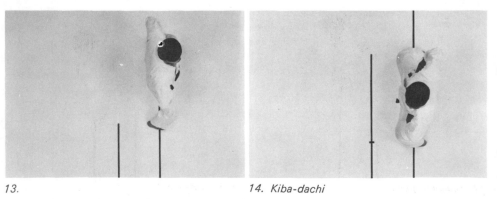

13.

14. *Kiba-dachi*

14 Hidari empi yoko uchi Jōtai sono mama

Side strike with left elbow/Upper body as before Do not change level of hips.

16 Migi empi yoko uchi

Side strike with right elbow Turn head to right. Do not change level of hips when raising knee.

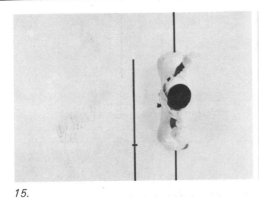

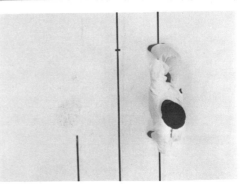

15.

16. Kiba-dachi

17 *Migi uraken migi sokumen tate mawashi-uchi*

18 *Hidari chūdan oi-zuki*

Vertical strike to right side with right back-fist

19 *Migi ken tsuki-age*
Hidari empi ushiro ate

Swinging punch with right fist/Strike to rear with left elbow

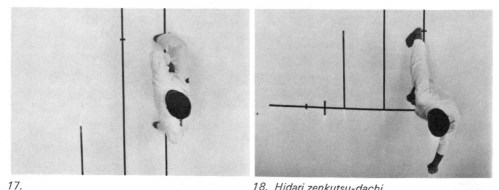

17.

18. *Hidari zenkutsu-dachi*

Bring right foot to left foot, then to the right and use it as pivot.

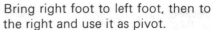

Left middle level lunge punch
Step in with left leg (*fumidashi*).

| 20 | *Hidari ken tsuki-age*
Migi empi ushiro ate |

YA!

Yame

Swinging punch with left fist/Strike to rear with right elbow *Yoriashi* to the right.

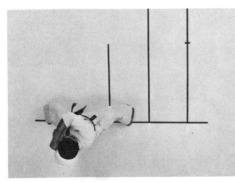

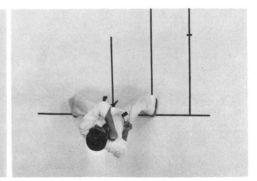

19. *Kiba-dachi*

20. *Kiba-dachi*

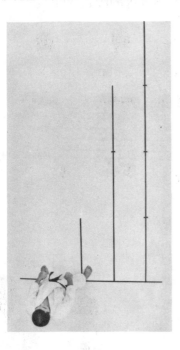

Heian 3 consists of changing blocks—from middle level to lower level—elbow block, back-fist strike, stamping kick and other techniques. Especially important are training in the straddle-leg stance and mastering the unique *tai-sabaki* of sliding the feet (*yori-ashi*).

Twenty movements. About forty seconds.

1

2

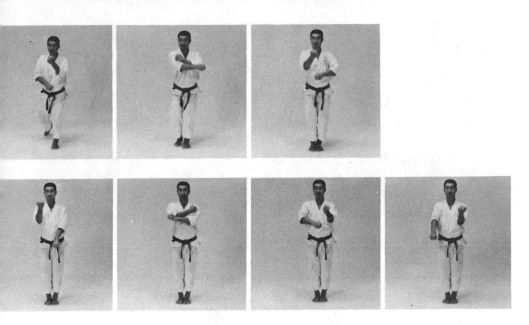

1. The fists in both the middle and lower level blocks should be equidistant from the body. Do not let either elbow move more than a fist-width from the side of the body. The fist for the middle level block, inside outward, passes outside the other elbow. Cross both arms in front of the chest to execute *kime*.

2. In the elbow block to the side of the body, the knee must be raised to chest level for the stamping kick (*fumikomi*). Do not block with the arm only. The feeling should be of blocking with the hips. Take advantage of the hip rotation, using hips, chest and both arms as a single, massive unit.

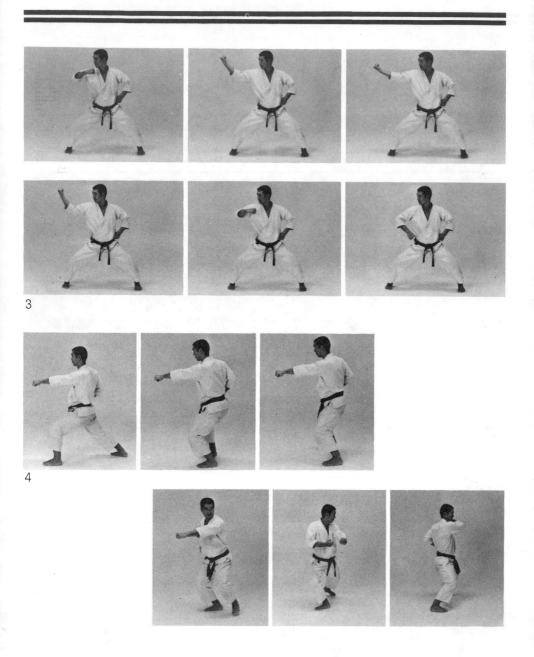

3. From elbow block to the side to vertical back-fist punch: Swing the fist from in front of the jaw and return the forearm along the same course, fist coming to the hip.

4. From left lunge punch to right swinging punch: Right foot is pivot. An elbow strike to the rear can be made at the same time.

$$\frac{4}{\text{HEIAN } 4}$$

1 *Hidari haiwan hidari sokumen jōdan yoko uke*
Migi zenwan hitai mae yoko kamae

Upper level block to left side with left back-arm/Right forearm at side of forehead kamae

3 *Ryō ken gedan jūji uke*

Lower level X block with both fists Thrust down from right shoulder and cross wrists.

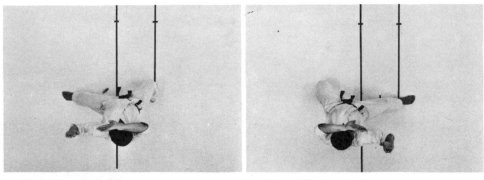

1. *Migi kōkutsu-dachi*   2. *Hidari kōkutsu-dachi*

2 *Migi haiwan migi sokumen jōdan yoko uke*
Hidari zenwan hitai mae yoko kamae

Upper level block to right side with right back-arm/Left forearm
at side of forehead kamae

4 *Migi chūdan morote uke* (*Migi chūdan uchi
uke/Hidari ken migi hiji-zoe*)

Right middle level augmented block (*Right middle level block,
inside outward/Left fist at right elbow*)

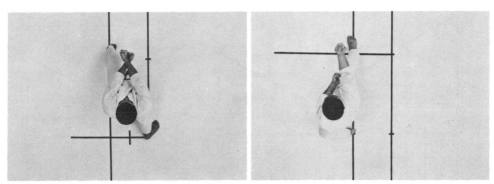

3. *Hidari zenkutsu-dachi*   4. *Hidari kōkutsu-dachi*

5 Ryō ken migi koshi kamae

Both fists at right side kamae

6 Hidari uraken hidari sokumen jōdan yoko mawashi-uchi/Hidari yoko keage

Upper level horizontal strike to left side with left back-fist/Left side snap kick

8 Ryō ken hidari koshi kamae

Both fists at left side kamae right. Turn head to right.

Bring left foot half a step to the

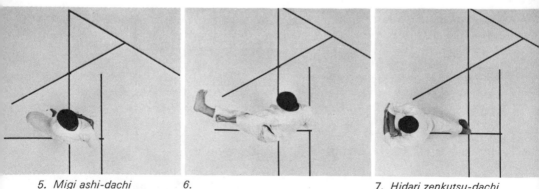

5. Migi ashi-dachi   6.   7. Hidari zenkutsu-dachi

7 Migi empi uchi

Right elbow strike Execute techniques 6 and 7 rapidly.
Strike left palm strongly.

9 Migi uraken migi sokumen jōdan yoko mawashi-uchi/Migi yoko keage   10 Hidari empi uchi

*Upper level horizontal strike to right side
with right back-fist/Right side snap kick*   *Left elbow strike*

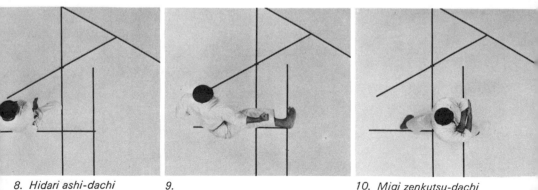

8. Hidari ashi-dachi   9.   10. Migi zenkutsu-dachi

11 Migi shutō jōdan yoko mawashi-uchi
Hidari shō jōdan uke

Upper level horizontal strike with right sword hand/Upper level block with left palm

14 Ryō ken chūdan kakiwake uke

Middle level reverse wedge block with both fists Execute this technique slowly.

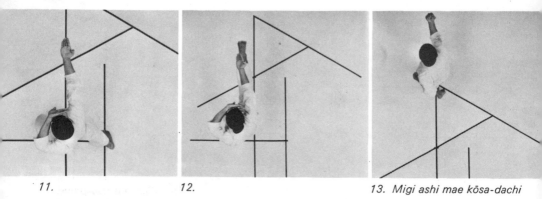

11.   12.   13. *Migi ashi mae kōsa-dachi*

12 *Migi jōdan mae keage*

Upper level right front snap kick

13 *Migi uraken tate mawashi-uchi Hidari ken hidari koshi*

Vertical strike with right back-fist/Left fist to left side

15 *Migi jōdan mae keage*

Upper level right front snap kick

16 *Migi chūdan oi-zuki Hidari ken hidari koshi*

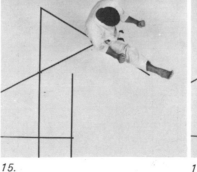

Right middle level lunge punch/Left fist to left side   Punch with return of foot to floor.

14. *Migi kōkutsu-dachi*   15.   16. *Migi zenkutsu-dachi*

17 *Hidari chūdan gyaku-zuki*

Left middle level reverse punch

18 *Chūdan kakiwake uke*

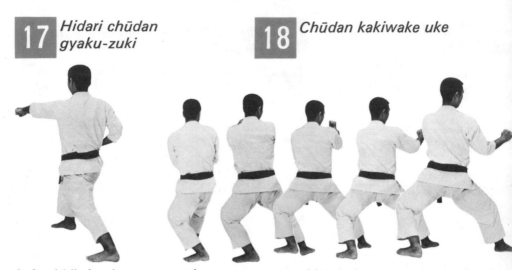

Middle level reverse wedge block

21 *Migi ken chūdan gyaku-zu-ki / Hidari ken hidari koshi*

Middle level reverse punch with right fist / Left fist to left side

22 *Hidari chūdan morote uke*

Left middle level augmented forearm block

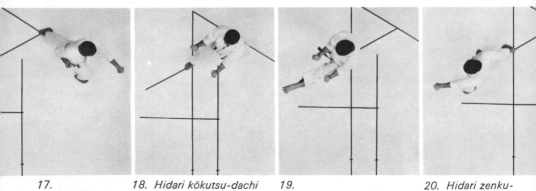

17.   18. *Hidari kōkutsu-dachi*   19.   20. *Hidari zenku-tsu-dachi*

19 Hidari jōdan mae keage

Upper level left front snap kick

20 Hidari ken chūdan oi-zuki

Middle level lunge punch with left fist

23 Migi chūdan morote uke

Right middle level augmented forearm block

24 Hidari chūdan morote uke

Left middle level augmented forearm block

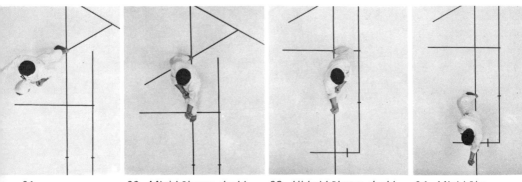

21.

22. Migi kōkutsu-dachi

23. Hidari kōkutsu-dachi

24. Migi kōku-tsu-dachi

71

25 *Migi hiza age-ate*
Ryō ken migi hiza ryōsoku hikioroshi

Right knee strike/Lower both fists at sides of right knee
Raise right knee high.

27 *Migi shutō chūdan uke*

Middle level block with right sword hand Keep hips at the
same level.

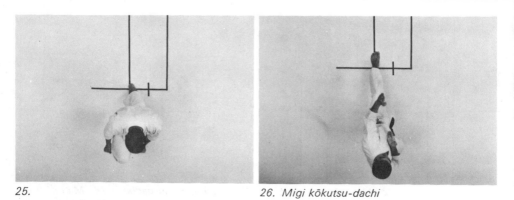

25.

26. *Migi kōkutsu-dachi*

26 *Hidari shutō chūdan uke* *Migi shutō mune mae kamae*

Middle level block with left sword hand/Right sword hand in front of chest kamae

Yame

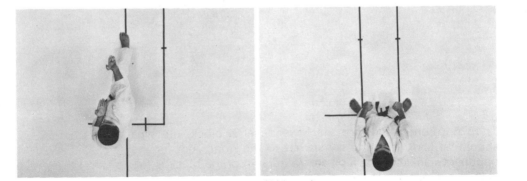

27. *Hidari kōkutsu-dachi*   *Shizen-tai*

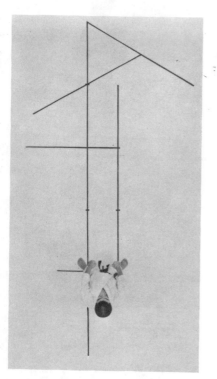

The techniques in Heian 4 are the downward X block and the middle level augmented forearm block, roundhouse sword hand strike, vertical elbow strike, reverse wedge block and knee strike. The difficult crossed-feet stance should be mastered. Movements 1 and 2 are done slowly, but hands and feet must move in unison.

Twenty-seven movements. About fifty seconds.

1

1. In the front stance for the lower level X block, the hips should be fairly low and somewhat to the front. Aim for the opponent's ankle. If the hips are withdrawn or the block is too high, it will not be effective.

2

3

2. In the upper level horizontal strike (movement 11), raise the left palm, bending the elbow, to the front of the forehead. Swing the right palm downward from the right side of the head in a wide arc. Both arms must be swung in unison with the leftward rotation of the hips.

3. In the vertical back-fist strike after the front kick, fully utilize the spring of the left ankle to jump in. Supporting the body weight on the right leg, bring the left foot behind the right ankle for the crossed-feet stance. This is necessary to maintain balance.

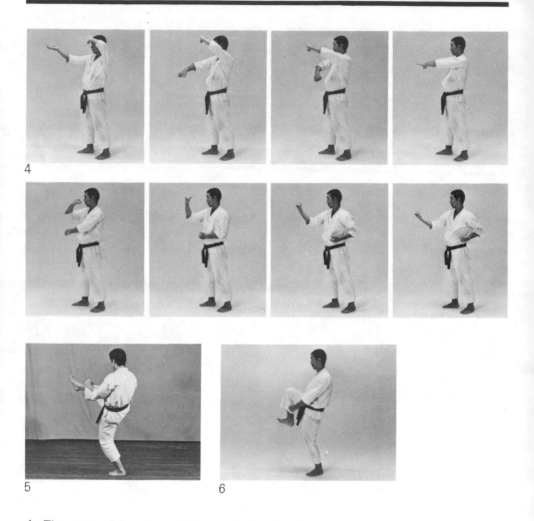

4

5

6

4. The essential point of the vertical strike is to swing the right hand in a wide arc as if following the course of the left hand. Strike to the front at jaw level at the same time the left fist is brought to the left hip.

5. When kicking after the middle level reverse wedge block, the armpits must be tight to keep the elbows near the body. Otherwise, the face and abdomen will be open to counterattack. At the same time the kicking leg is lowered, continuous punches can be executed.

6. Rising knee strike after augmented forearm block from right back stance: Bend front knee and shift weight forward without raising hips. Raise both hands diagonally, then immediately raise right knee high and bring both hands down to the side of the leg.

HEIAN $\dfrac{5}{5}$

1 *Hidari ken chūdan uchi uke*

Middle level block, inside outward, with left fist   Execute techniques 1 and 2 rapidly.

3 *Hidari zenwan mizu-nagare kamae*

Left forearm flowing water position   Move head, arms and leg together and slowly.

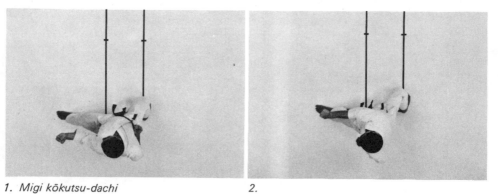

1. Migi kōkutsu-dachi   2.

2 Migi ken chūdan gyaku-zuki

Middle level reverse punch with right fist Withdraw left fist strongly.

4 Migi ken chūdan uchi uke

5 Hidari ken chūdan gyaku-zuki

Middle level block, inside outward, with right fist *Middle level reverse punch with left fist*

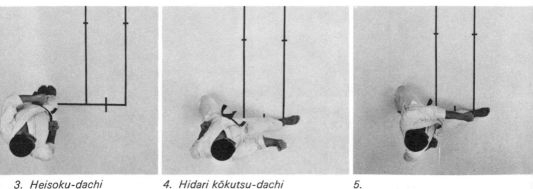

3. Heisoku-dachi   4. Hidari kōkutsu-dachi   5.

Migi zenwan mizu-nagare kamae

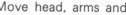

Right forearm flowing water position Move head, arms and
leg together and slowly.

Ryō ken gedan jūji uke

Lower level X block with both fists Cross wrists while advanc-
ing left leg.

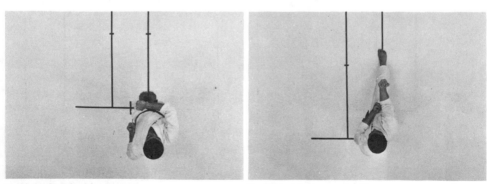

6. *Heisoku-dachi*   7. *Hidari kōkutsu-dachi*

7 Migi chūdan morote uke

Right middle level augmented forearm block

9 Ryō shō jōdan jūji uke

Upper level X block with both palms Thrust upwards with wrists still crossed.

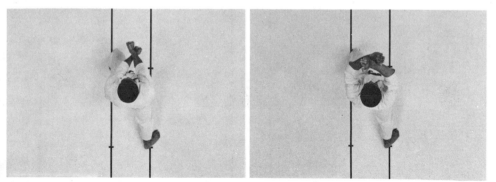

8. Hidari zenkutsu-dachi   9.

10 | *Ryō shō chūdan osae-uke*

Middle level pressing block with both palms Keep wrists together. Extend right hand.

13 | **Migi ken migi sokumen gedan barai**

Downward block to right side with right fist Bring right fist about 5 centimeters above right knee.

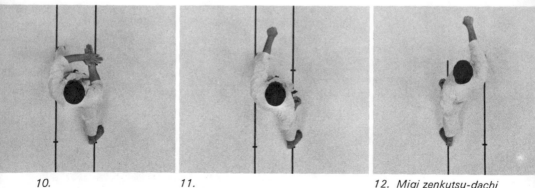

10.

11.

12. Migi zenkutsu-dachi

11 *Hidari ken chūdan-zuki* ## 12 *Migi ken chūdan oi-zuki* **EI!**

Middle level punch with left fist   *Middle level straight punch with right fist*

14 *Hidari shō hidari sokumen chūdan kake-uke*

Middle level hooking block to left side with left palm Bring
left palm forward from under right elbow.

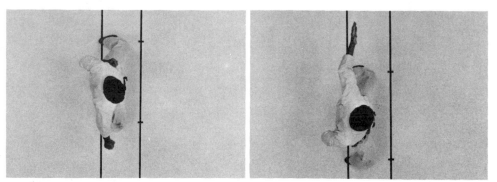

13. Kiba-dachi   14.

15 Migi mikazuki-geri

Right crescent kick Kick left palm with right sole, quickly return foot to right side.

17 Migi chūdan morote uke

Right middle level augmented forearm block Bend right knee. Bring left foot behind right foot.

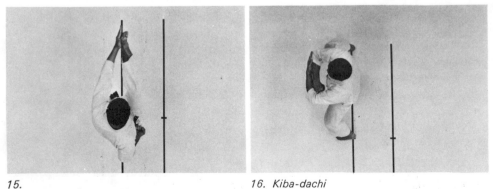

15.

16. Kiba-dachi

16 *Migi empi mae uchi*

Front strike with right elbow   Keep left hand in the same place.

18 *Migi morote kōhō tsuki-age*

Right augmented swinging punch to the rear   Keep left fist at right elbow.

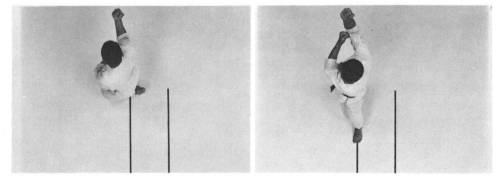

17. *Migi ashi mae kōsa-dachi*   18. *Renoji-dachi*

19 *Ryō ken gedan jūji uke*

Downward X block with both fists

21
a *Migi shutō gedan uchi-komi*
Hidari shō migi kata ue nagashi-uke

Downward strike with right sword hand/Sweeping block, left palm to right shoulder

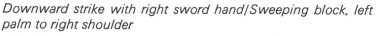

19. *Migi ashi mae kōsa-dachi*   20. *Migi zenkutsu-dachi*

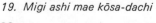

20 *Migi chūdan morote uke*

Right middle level augmented forearm block Straighten left knee. Slide right foot to the right.

21 b *Migi ken migi sokumen jōdan uchi uke*
Hidari ken migi sokumen gedan uke

Upper level block, inside outward, to right side with right fist/Downward block to right side with left fist

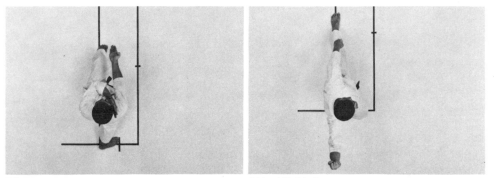

21a.

21b. *Migi kōkutsu-dachi*

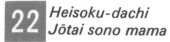

22 Heisoku-dachi
Jōtai sono mama

Informal attention stance/Upper body as before Slide left foot slowly next to right foot.

23 b Hidari ken hidari sokumen jōdan uchi uke
Migi ken migi sokumen gedan uke

Upper level block, inside outward, to left side with left fist
Downward block to right side with right fist

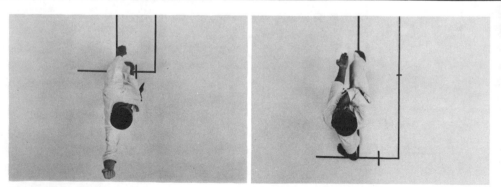

22. Heisoku-dachi   23a. Migi zenkutsu-dachi

23

a *Hidari shutō gedan uchi-komi*
Migi shō hidari kata ue nagashi-uke

Downward strike with left sword hand/Sweeping block, right palm to left shoulder

Yame

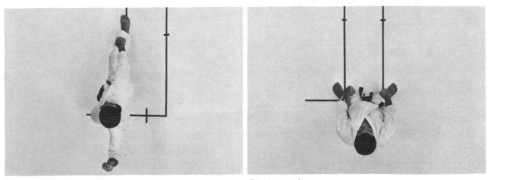

23b.   Shizen-tai

The techniques in Heian 5 include the flowing water position, upper level X block, middle level pressing block with both palms, downward block to the side from the straddle-leg stance, middle level hooking block to the side, crescent kick and crossed-feet stance after jumping. In going from the middle level reverse punch from the back stance to the informal attention stance-flowing water position (movements 2–3 and 5–6), head, arms and leg must move in coordination with the hip rotation. When this is mastered, movements 10, 11 and 12 can be executed continuously. In movement 19, the crossed-feet stance after jumping must be strong. This stance occurs often in the kata.

Twenty-three movements. About fifty seconds.

1

1. In going from the lower level X block to the upper level X block, keep the wrists crossed, bring both palms close to the chest, and block by thrusting upward. Then extend the right palm in front of the right nipple, palm upward. Turn left palm downward.

2

2. Downward side block: Turn hips and head to the left and bend left knee. While raising left palm to right shoulder, strike downward with right palm. Without moving feet, shift weight to right leg. As if wringing out a towel, block diagonally downward with the left fist while raising the right fist above and in back of the right shoulder.

3

3. Point 2 applies also in movements 22–23. Take care to not move feet while shifting from front to back stance.

6
TEKKI 1

1 *Kao migi muki*
Jōtai sono mama

Turn head to right/Upper body as is Lower hips. Cross left
foot over right.

3 *Hidari empi migi sokumen chūdan uchi*
Migi shō hidari hiji ate

*Middle level strike to right side with left elbow/Right palm to
left elbow*

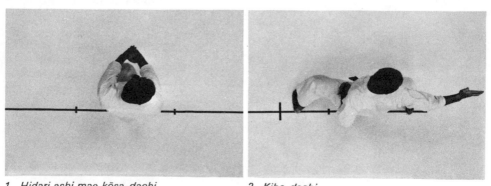

1. Hidari ashi mae kōsa-dachi   *2. Kiba-dachi*

94

2
Migi shō migi sokumen chūdan kake-uke
Hidari ken hidari koshi

Middle level hooking block to right side with right palm/Left fist to left side

4
Ryō ken migi koshi kamae
Kao hidari muki

Both fists right side kamae/Turn head to left Back of left fist to the front, back of right, downward.

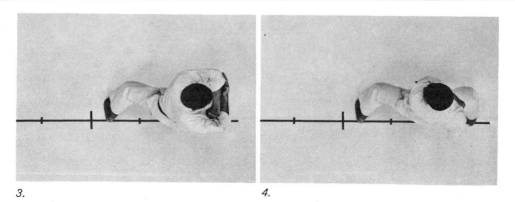

3.   4.

5 | *Hidari gedan barai*

Left downward block The feeling is of blocking an attack to the left side strongly.

7 | *Migi ashi mae kōsa-dachi*
Jōtai sono mama

Right foot in front, crossed-feet stance/Upper body as before Do not break posture of torso.

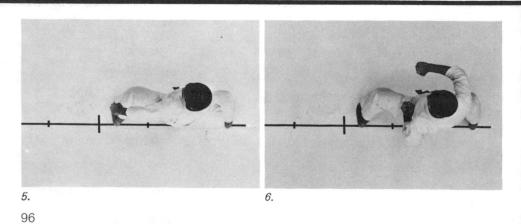

5.   6.

6 Migi ken kagi-zuki

Hook punch with right fist Bring right forearm about 20 centimeters in front of and parallel to the chest.

8 Migi chūdan uchi uke
Kao shōmen muki

Right middle level block, inside outward/Turn face to front Strong stamping kick to the left.

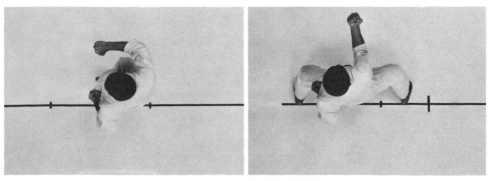

7. Migi ashi mae kōsa-dachi

8. Kiba-dachi

9 a
Hidari haiwan jōdan nagashi-uke / Migi gedan uke

Upper level sweeping block with left back-arm / Right downward block

9 b
Hidari ken jōdan ura-zuki

Upper level close punch with left fist / Right fist at left elbow

11 b
Hidari ude hidari sokumen chūdan uke

Middle level block to left side with left arm

12
Kao migi muki Jōtai sono mama

Turn head to left / Upper body as before

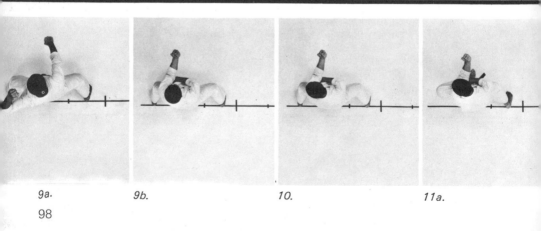

9a.　　　　9b.　　　　10.　　　　11a.

10 *Kao hidari muki
Jōtai sono mama*

Turn head to right/Upper body as
before

**11**
a *Hidari ashi nami-gaeshi
Jōtai sono mama*

Left returning wave kick/Upper body as
before

13
a *Migi ashi nami-gaeshi
Jōtai sono mama*

Right returning wave kick/Upper body
as before

13
b *Hidari ude migi sokumen
chūdan uke*

Middle level block to right side with left
arm   Keep right fist at left elbow.

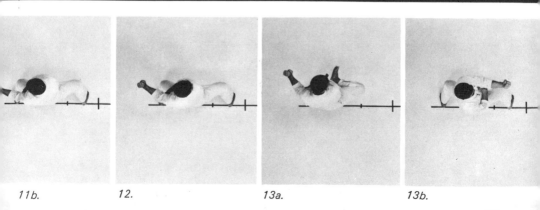

11b.   12.   13a.   13b.

14 *Ryō ken migi koshi kamae*
Kao hidari muki

Both fists right side kamae/Turn head to left   Move head and arms simultaneously.

16 *Hidari shō hidari sokumen chūdan kake-uke*
Migi ken migi koshi

Middle level hooking block to left side with left palm/Right fist to right side

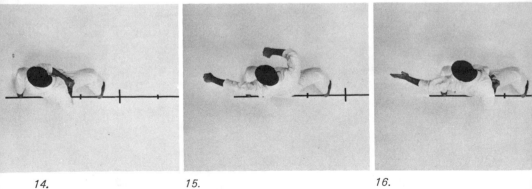

14.   15.   16.

15 Hidari ken hidari sokumen chūdan-zuki
Migi ken chūdan kagi-zuki

EI!

Middle level punch to left side with left fist/Middle level hook punch with right fist

17 Migi empi hidari sokumen chūdan uchi

Middle level strike to left side with right elbow

18 Ryō ken hidari koshi kamae

Both fists left side kamae
Turn head to right

19 Migi gedan barai

Right downward block

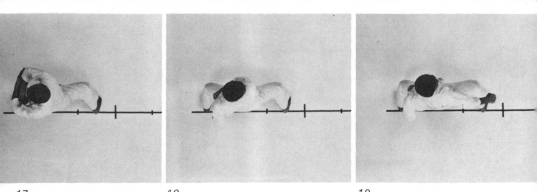

17.   18.   19.

20 *Hidari ken kagi-zuki*

Hook punch with left fist

21 *Hidari ashi mae kōsa-dachi*

Left foot in front, crossed-feet stance

23 a *Migi haiwan jōdan nagashi-uke/Hidari gedan uke*

Upper level sweeping block with right back-arm/Left downward block

23 b *Migi ken jōdan ura-zuki*

Upper level close punch with right fist

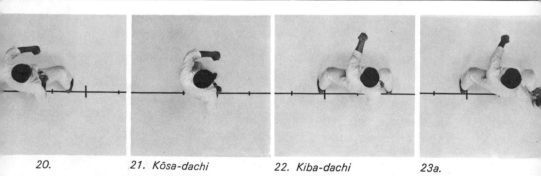

20.   21. Kōsa-dachi   22. Kiba-dachi   23a.

22 Hidari chūdan uchi uke
Kao shōmen muki

Left middle level block, inside outward/Turn face to front

24 Kao migi muki

25a Migi ashi na-mi-gaeshi

25b Migi ude migi sokumen chū-dan uke

Turn face to right

Right returning wave kick

Middle level block to right side with right arm

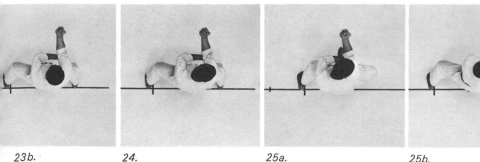

23b.　　　24.　　　25a.　　　25b.

103

26 *Kao hidari muki*
Jōtai sono mama

Turn head to left/Upper body as before

27_a *Hidari ashi nami-gaeshi*

Left returning wave kick

29 *Migi ken migi sokumen chūdan-zuki*
Hidari ken kagi-zuki

Middle level punch to right side with right fist/Hook punch with
left fist

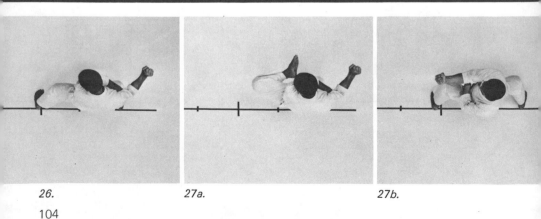

26.   27a.   27b.

27 b Migi ude hidari sokumen chūdan uke

Middle level block to left side with right arm   Strong *fumikomi*.

28 Ryō ken hidari koshi kamae Kao migi muki

Both fists at left side kamae/Turn head to right

Yame

Quietly face to front and slowly return arms and legs to original *kamae*.

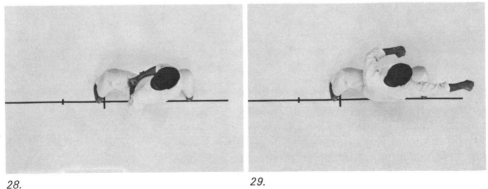

28.

29.

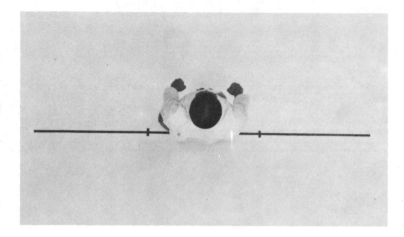

The performance line in the Tekki kata is a straight line, with movements being made to one side or the other. If the crossed-feet stance is not correct, the performance line tends to bend to the front. So the timing of shifting the body weight and aligning the toes of both feet is important. Whatever the movement, the straddle-leg stance should not be broken. And when executing techniques to the side, the body from the hips down must face forward. Since these kata are rather monotonous, turn the head briskly and strongly.

Twenty-nine movements. About fifty seconds.

1

1. Most important is the hook punch. By executing this correctly, the tightening of the shoulders, elbows and armpits can be mastered. This in turn should lead to development in punching and effective blocking. A remarkable difference in the use of techniques can result from learning this kata.

2

3

2. In the stamping kick from the straddle-leg stance, keep the left knee taut even as the body weight gradually shifts to the right. Bring the right foot from behind the left knee, raising the knee in a high arch.

3. In the returning wave kick, the position of the hips must not change.

4

4. From upper level sweeping forearm block to upper level close punch: Raise the right fist from under the left elbow to the right ear. At the same time, bring the left fist from the right shoulder downward and outward. Then strike straight to the front with the right fist, the left fist coming below the right elbow.

7
TEKKI 2

1 *Ryō hiji suihei ni haru*
Kao migi muki

Elbows horizontally spread/Turn head to right Do this slowly
and quietly. ·

3 *Migi zenwan shōmen gedan uke*
Hidari shō migi hiji ni soeru

*Lower level block to the front with right forearm/Left palm sup-
porting right elbow*

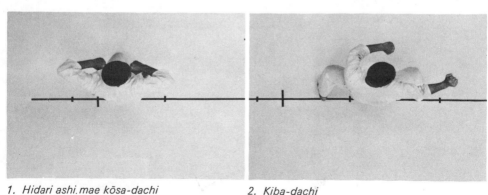

1. *Hidari ashi mae kōsa-dachi*
2. *Kiba-dachi*

2 *Migi zenwan migi sokumen chūdan uke*
Hidari zenwan mune mae suihei kamae

Middle level block to right side with right forearm/Left forearm horizontal kamae

4 *Migi zenwan migi sokumen gedan uke*
Hidari shō migi hiji ni soeta mama

Lower level block to right side with right forearm/Left palm supporting right elbow

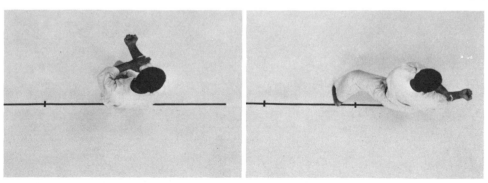

3. *Hidari ashi mae kōsa-dachi*   4. *Kiba-dachi*

5

Ryō hiji suihei ni haru
Kao hidari muki

Elbows horizontally spread/Turn head to left Move left leg
and arms simultaneously.

7 *Hidari zenwan shōmen gedan uke*
Migi shō hidari hiji ni soeru

Lower level block to front with left forearm/Right palm support-
ing left elbow

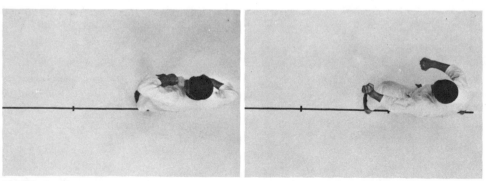

5. Heisoku-dachi

6. Kiba-dachi

Hidari zenwan hidari sokumen chūdan uke
Migi zenwan mune mae suihei kamae

Middle level block to left side with left forearm/Right forearm
horizontal kamae

8 *Hidari zenwan hidari sokumen gedan uke*
Migi shō hidari hiji ni soeta mama

Lower level block to left side with left forearm/Right palm
supporting left elbow

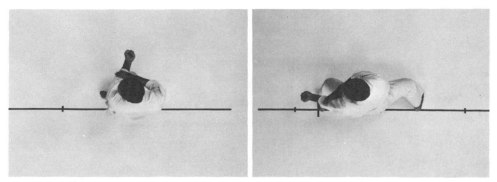

7. *Migi ashi mae kōsa-dachi*   8. *Kiba-dachi*

9 *Hidari shō hidari koshi*
Migi ken hidari shō ni ateru

Left palm at left side/Right fist to left palm Back of left hand
outward, back of right fist to the front.

11 **a** *Migi ken migi koshi/Hidari shō migi ken mae ni ateru*

11 **b** *Migi empi uchi/Hidari shō suigetsu mae ni tateru*

Right fist at right side/Left palm in front of right fist

Right elbow strike/Left palm vertical in front of chest

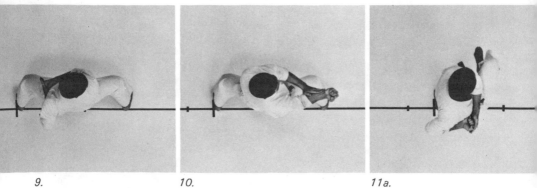

9.   10.   11a.

10 *Migi zenwan migi sokumen chūdan uke*
Hidari shō migi tekubi ni soeru

Middle level block to right side with right forearm/Left palm at right wrist

12 *Migi shō migi sokumen chūdan tsukami-uke/Kao migi muki*

 **13** *Hidari ken kagi-zuki*

Middle level grasping block to right side with right fist/Turn head to right

Hook punch with left fist

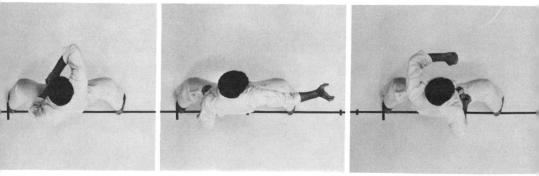

11b. Kiba-dachi   *12.*   *13.*

14 *Hidari ashi mae kōsa-dachi*

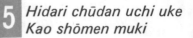 **15** *Hidari chūdan uchi uke*
Kao shōmen muki

Left foot in front, crossed-feet stance

Left middle level block, inside outward
Turn face to front

 17 *Migi shō migi koshi / Hidari ken migi shō ni ateru*
Kao hidari muki

Right palm at right side / Left fist to right palm / Turn face to left

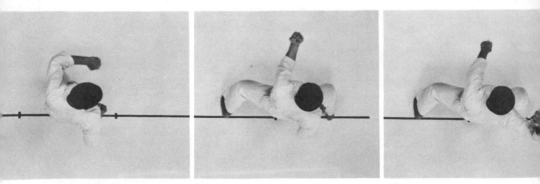

14. Kōsa-dachi   15. Kiba-dachi   16a.

16 a *Migi haiwan jōdan na-gashi-uke/Hidari ken ge-dan uke*

16 b *Migi ken jōdan ura-zuki Hidari zenwan mune mae suihei kamae*

Upper level sweeping block with right back-arm/Downward block with left fist

Upper level close punch with right fist/Left forearm horizontal kamae

18 *Hidari zenwan hidari sokumen chūdan uke Migi shō hidari tekubi ni soeru*

Middle level block to left side with left forearm/Right palm to left wrist

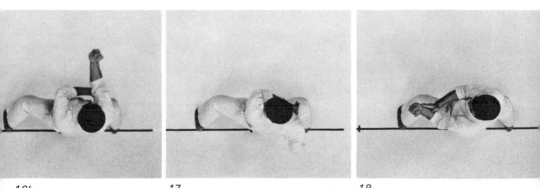

16b.   17.   18.

19 a

Hidari ken hidari koshi Migi shō hidari ken mae

Left fist at left side/Right palm in front of left fist

19 b

Hidari empi uchi/Migi shō suigetsu mae ni tateru

Left elbow strike/Right palm vertically in front of chest

21 *Migi ken kagi-zuki*

Hook punch with right fist

22 *Migi ashi mae kōsa-dachi*

Right foot in front, crossed-feet stance

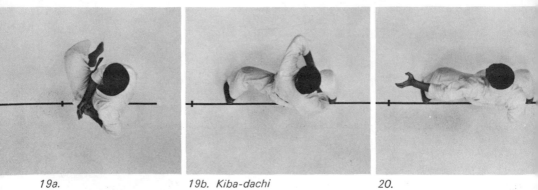

19a.

19b. Kiba-dachi

20.

118

20 Hidari shō hidari sokumen chūdan tsukami-uke

Middle level grasping block to left side with left palm Slowly.

23 Migi chūdan uchi uke

Right middle level block, inside outward

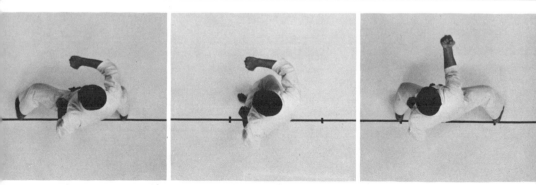

21.

22. Migi ashi mae kōsa-dachi

23. Kiba-dachi

24 a *Hidari haiwan jōdan na-gashi-uke/Migi gedan uke*

Upper level sweeping block with left back-arm/Right lower level block

Yame

24 b *Hidari ken jōdan ura-zuki/ Migi zenwan mune mae suihei kamae*

Upper level close punch with left fist Right forearm horizontal kamae

Quietly withdraw right leg to return to *shizen-tai*.

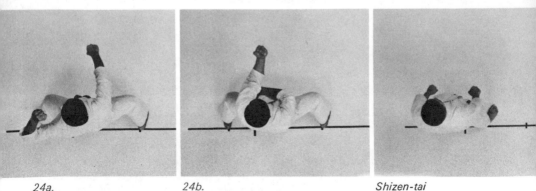

24a.   *24b.*   *Shizen-tai*

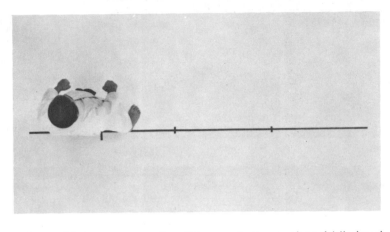

From this kata, master the difference between the middle level grasping block (*tsukami-uke*) and hooking block (*kake-uke*). *Twenty-four movements. About fifty seconds.*

1. Movements 1 and 2: Raise the forearms in front of the head with the feeling of folding the shoulders together. Block strongly to the right with the elbow bent.

121

2

3

4

2. In the lower level block to the front while moving to the side, bringing the right arm down must be done at the same time the left foot is brought in front of the right foot. The foot movement is slow and smooth, the arm movement forceful.

3. Elbow strike to the front (movements 10–11): To be effective, the hands must come to the side simultaneously with the raising of the knee and the strike be made while bringing the leg down. The upper body turns, but the hips and legs should face to the front throughout the movement.

4. In contrast to the sword hand and slightly "rising" wrist of the hooking block (see Vol. 1, p. 61), open the thumb and swing the arm in a half circle for the grasping block, lightly bending the elbow in the final phase. Tighten the armpits while drawing the opponent towards you.

$$\frac{8}{3}$$ TEKKI

1

Hidari chūdan uchi uke
Migi ken migi koshi

Left middle level block, inside outward/Right fist at right side

3

Migi zenwan chūdan barai
Hidari zenwan mune mae suihei kamae

*Middle level block with right forearm/Left forearm horizontal
kamae* Right elbow on left wrist.

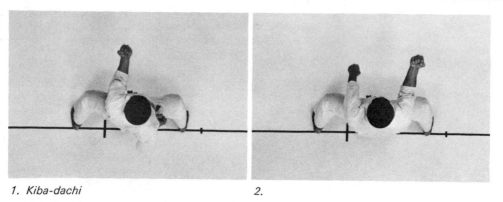

1. Kiba-dachi   2.

2 Migi chūdan uchi uke
Hidari gedan uke

Right middle level block, inside outward/Left downward block

4 Migi haiwan jōdan nagashi-uke
Hidari ude wa sono mama

Upper level sweeping block with right back-arm/Left arm as is

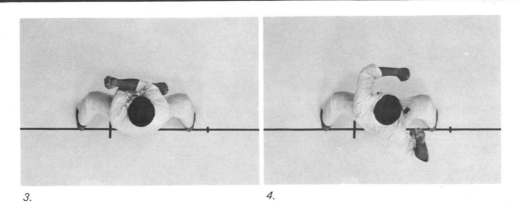

3.   4.

5 | *Migi ken jōdan ura-zuki*

Upper level close punch with right fist Bring right elbow on top of left fist.

7 | **Migi ken chūdan choku-zuki**
Hidari ude wa sono mama

Middle level straight punch with right fist/Left arm as is

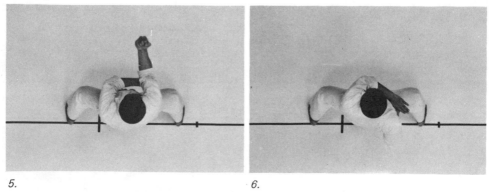

5.   6.

6

Migi ken migi koshi
Hidari shō migi ken ue

Right fist at right side/Left palm on right fist Back of right fist and left palm downward.

8

Migi zenwan hineri
Kao migi muki

Twist right forearm/Turn head to right No power in right elbow.

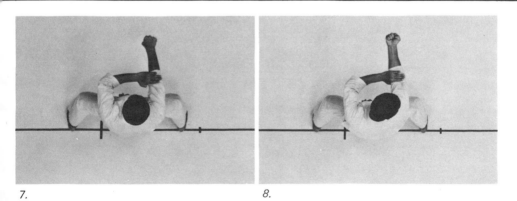

7.   8.

9 *Hidari ashi mae kōsa-dachi*
Jōtai sono mama

Left foot in front, crossed-feet stance/Upper body as before

11 *Migi ken migi sokumen gedan furisute*
Hidari shō soeta mama

Lower level swing to right side with right fist/Left palm as is

9. *Hidari ashi mae-kōsa-dachi*   10. *Kiba-dachi*

10 *Migi zenwan migi sokumen gedan oshi-uke*
Hidari shō migi hiji ni soeru

Lower level pressing block to right side with right forearm/Left palm supporting right elbow

12 *Migi ken migi koshi-biki*
Hidari shō migi ken ura ue-zoe

Pull right fist to right side/Left palm on right fist

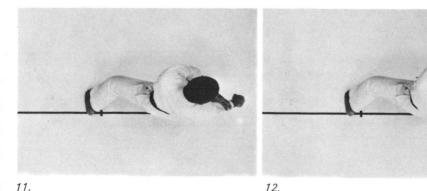

11.   12.

13 *Migi ken chūdan choku-zuki*
Hidari shō sono mama

Middle level straight punch with right fist/Left palm as is Twist
right arm while thrusting it forward.

15 *Hidari chūdan uchi uke*
Migi gedan uke

Left middle level block, inside outward/Right lower level block

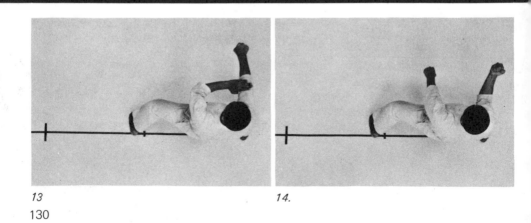

13 *14.*

14 *Migi chūdan uchi uke*
Hidari gedan uke

Right middle level block, inside outward/Left lower level block

16 a *Hidari haiwan jōdan nagashi-uke/Migi ken sono mama*

16 b *Hidari ken jōdan ura-zuki/Migi zenwan mune mae suihei kamae*

Upper level sweeping block with left back-arm/Right fist as is

Upper level close punch with left fist/Right forearm horizontal kamae

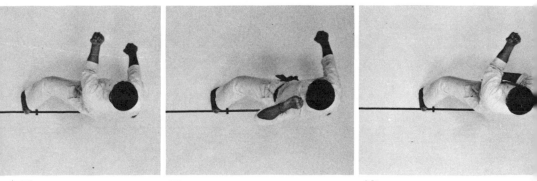

15.   16a.   16b.

17 *Kao hidari muki*
Jōtai sono mama

Turn head to left/Upper body as
before

18 *Migi ashi mae kōsa-dachi*
Jōtai sono mama

Right foot in front, crossed-feet stance
Upper body as before

20 *Hidari zenwan chūdan barai*
Migi ude wa sono mama

Middle level block with left forearm
Right arm as is

21 *Hidari haiwan jōdan*
nagashi-uke

Upper level sweeping block with
left back-arm

17.

18. *Migi ashi mae kōsa-dachi*

19. *Kiba-dachi*

19 *Kao shōmen muki/Hidari fumikomi Jōtai sono mama*

Turn head to front/Left stamping kick/Upper body as before.

22 *Hidari ken jōdan ura-zuki*

Upper level close punch with left fist

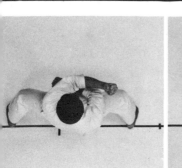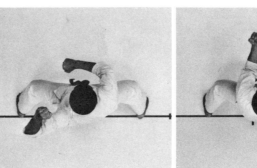

20.   21.   22.

23
**Hidari ken hidari koshi
Migi shō hidari ken ue**

Left fist at left side/Right palm on left fist

24
**Hidari ken chūdan choku-zuki
Migi shō sono mama**

Middle level straight punch with left fist/Right palm as is

27
**Hidari zenwan hidari sokumen gedan oshi-uke
Migi shō hidari hiji-zoe**

Lower level pressing block to left side with left forearm/Right palm supporting left elbow

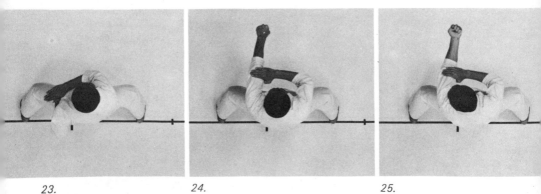

23.

24.

25.

25 *Kao hidari muki/Hidari zen-wan hineri*

Turn head to left/Turn left fist over

26 *Migi ashi mae kōsa-dachi*

Right foot in front, crossed-feet stance

28 *Hidari ken hidari sokumen gedan furisute Migi shō soeta mama*

Lower level swing to left side with left fist/Right palm supporting left elbow

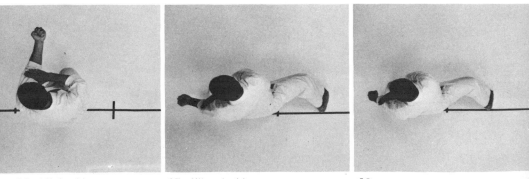

26. *Migi ashi mae kōsa-dachi*   27. *Kiba-dachi*   28.

29
**Hidari ken hidari koshi ni hiku
Migi shō hidari ken ue-zoe**

30
**Hidari ken chūdan
choku-zuki**

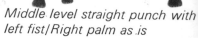

Pull left fist to left side/Right palm on left fist

Middle level straight punch with left fist/Right palm as is

32
**Hidari ken kagi-zuki
Migi ken migi koshi**

Hook punch with left fist/Right fist at right side

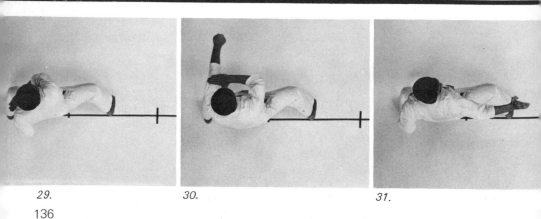

29.

30.

31.

31 *Migi shō migi sokumen chūdan tsukami-uke*
Hidari ken hidari koshi ni hiku

Middle level grasping block to right side with right palm
Withdraw left fist to left side

33 *Hidari ashi mae kōsa-dachi*
Jōtai sono mama

Left foot in front, crossed-feet stance/Upper body as before

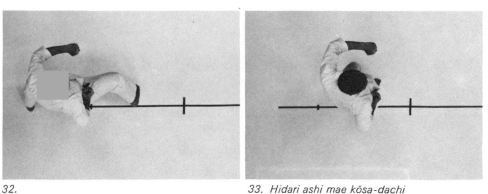

32.

33. *Hidari ashi mae kōsa-dachi*

34 *Hidari chūdan uchi uke/Migi ken sono mama*
Kao shōmen muki

Left middle level block, inside outward/Right fist as is/Turn head to front

36 *Migi ken jōdan ura-zuki*
Hidari zenwan mune mae suihei kamae

Upper level close punch with right fist/Left forearm horizontal kamae

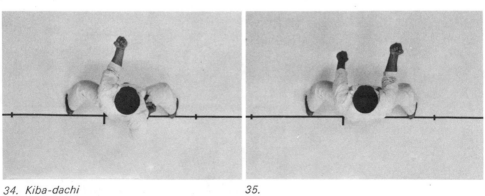

34. Kiba-dachi   *35.*

35 Migi chūdan uchi uke
Hidari gedan uke

Right middle level block, inside outward/Left lower level block

Yame

Withdraw right leg and quietly return to *shizen-tai*.

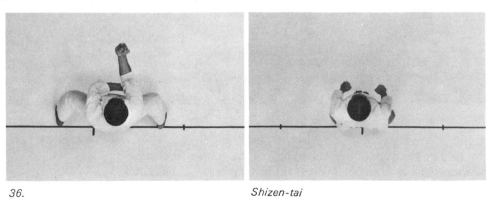

36.   *Shizen-tai*

Mastery of quick timing is necessary for the changing blocks. Master the straddle-leg and crossed-feet stances.
Thirty-six movements. About fifty seconds.

1

1. Except for stance, the changing middle-lower level blocks are the same as in Heian 3. Blocking in movement 3 is like striking to the left.

2

2. In the downward swing (movement 11), the arm is brought back to the same position, but with the back of the hand upward. Do not let the torso wiggle.

GLOSSARY

Roman numerals refer to other volumes in this series: I, Comprehensive; II, Fundamentals; III, Kumite 1; IV, Kumite 2.

age-uke: rising block, 20, 28, 44; I, 70; II, 90, 118

ashi: foot, leg

choku-zuki: straight punch, 28, 126; I, 66; II, 102; IV, 62

chūdan: middle level

chūdan barai: middle level block, 124

chūdan uchi: middle level strike, 94

chūdan uke: middle level block, 28, 73, 98, 111; I, 59, 96; II, 90, 106

chūdan-zuki: middle level punch, 32, 83, 101

dan: 13

embusen: performance line, 13, 106; I, 94

empi: elbow

empi mae uchi: elbow strike to the front, 85, 122

empi uchi: elbow strike, 67; I, 77

empi ushiro ate: elbow strike to the rear, 58

fumidashi: 58; II, 68

fumikomi: stamping kick, 60, 61, 97, 105, 107, 133; II, 60, 68; III, 33

furisute: swing, 128, 141

gedan: lower level

gedan barai: downward block, 17, 28, 43, 82, 90, 96, 122; I, 56; II, 106

gedan uke: downward block, 50, 87, 91, 98, 110, 125

gyaku hanmi: reverse half-front-facing position, 40, 46, 48; II, 24

gyaku-zuki: reverse punch, 40, 48, 70, 79, 90; I, 68; II, 124; IV, 108

hachinoji-dachi: open-leg stance, 16; I, 29

haiwan: upper side of forearm, back-arm

heisoku-dachi: informal attention stance, 50, 79, 88, 90, 112; I, 29

hidari: left

hidari ashi-dachi: left leg stance, 35, 67

hiji: elbow

hiji uke: elbow block, 60, 61, 62

hitai: forehead

hiza age-ate: rising knee strike, 72, 74, 76

ikken hissatsu: to kill with one blow, 11

jiku ashi: pivot leg, 17, 19, 22, 29, 30; II, 60; III, 72, 100

jōdan: upper level

jōdan uke: upper level block, 46, 68; I, 57; II, 106

jōtai: upper body

jūji uke: X block, 64, 74, 80, 90; I, 64

kagi-zuki: hook punch, 97, 106, 115, 136; I, 71; II, 90

kake-uke: hooking block, 83, 90, 95, 121, 122; I, 61

kakiwake uke: reverse wedge block, 68, 74, 76; I, 64

kamae: posture, 12, 32, 46, 105; III, 14, 21, 26, 36, 40; IV, 40

kata: shoulder

ken: fist

kentsui: hammer fist, 18; I, 17

kiai: 14

kiba-dachi: straddle-leg stance, 54, 60, 83, 94, 106, 110, 124, 140; I, 32; II, 52

kime: finish, 11, 61; I, 50; III, 15, 34; IV, 118

kōhō tenkan: reversing direction, 29,
30, 46; II, 72; III, 100
kōkutsu-dachi: back stance, 26, 28,
30, 32, 50, 64, 78; I, 31; II, 52; III,
40, 54
kōsa-dachi: crossed-feet stance, 68,
74, 75, 85, 90, 94, 96, 106, 110, 116,
128, 140; II, 52
koshi: hip, side; I, 52; II, 13
koshi no kaiten: hip rotation, 61, 75;
II, 16
kumite: sparring, 10, 13; I, 111
kyū: 13

mae: front
mae keage: front snap kick, 41, 46,
48, 69, 75; I, 86; II, 88; III, 67, 98
mawarikomi: circling, 29; IV, 98
migi: right
migi ashi-dachi: right leg stance, 66
mikazuki-geri: crescent kick, 84, 90;
IV, 52, 54
mizu-nagare kamae: flowing water
position, 78, 90; I, 104; II, 90; IV,
122
morote kōhō tsuki-age: augmented
swinging punch to the rear, 85
morote uke: augmented forearm block,
42, 52, 65, 74, 76, 81; I, 64
mune: chest
musubi-dachi: informal attention
stance, toes out, 12; I, 29

nagashi-uke: sweeping block, 33, 86,
98, 108, 117, 125; I, 62; IV, 82
nami-gaeshi: returning wave kick, 99,
107; I, 106
nukite: spear hand

oi-zuki: lunge punch, 16, 28, 55, 62,
69, 83; I, 68; II, 88, 126; III, 34, 136
osae-uke: pressing block, 37, 53, 82,
90; I, 62, 64
oshi-uke: pressing block, 129

renoji-dachi: L stance, 85; I, 29
ren-zuki: alternate punching, 76; I,
68
ryō: both

shihon nukite: four-finger spear hand
shizen-tai: natural position, 16, 28;
I, 28
shō: palm
shōmen: front

shutō: sword hand
shutō mawashi uchi: roundhouse
sword hand strike, 68; I, 74, 82; II,
130; III, 72, 78, 79, 104, 116
shutō uke: sword hand block, 26, 28,
36; I, 60; II, 118; IV, 138
sokumen: side
sokutō: sword foot
suigetsu: solar plexus, chest
sun-dome: arresting a technique, 11

tai-sabaki: 60; II, 76–79; III, 15, 72,
80, 100, 114, 128; IV, 86, 102
tanden: center of gravity, 12
tate mawashi hiji uchi: vertical elbow
strike, 74; I, 24; II, 131; III, 84
tate mawashi-uchi: vertical strike, 18,
56, 62, 69, 76; I, 75; II, 129
tate-zuki: vertical punch, 37, 53; I, 70
tekubi: wrist
tsukami-uke: grasping block, 115,
121, 122, 137
tsuki-age: swinging punch, 58, 62

uchi-komi: strike, 33, 86
uchi uke: block, inside outward, 40,
48, 50, 61, 78, 87, 97, 116, 124; I,
59; II, 22
ude: arm
uke-gae: changing blocks, 60, 61,
140
uraken: back-fist
uraken-uchi: back-fist strike, 46, 47,
60, 75; I, 74, 75; II, 82; III, 76, 80,
106; IV, 108, 112
ura-zuki: close punch, 98, 108, 117,
126; I, 70; IV, 44
ushiro: rear

yame: stop
yoko keage: side snap kick, 35, 46, 47,
66; I, 87; II, 135
yoko mawashi-uchi: horizontal strike,
35, 54, 66, 75; I, 75; II, 129
yoko uchi: side strike, 55
yoko uke: side block 32, 64
yori-ashi: sliding the feet, 60; II, 70;
III, 100, 117

zanshin: state of relaxed alertness, 12;
III, 26
zenkutsu-dachi: front stance, 17, 28,
37, 53, 65, 81; I, 30; II, 18, 52
zenwan: forearm